This Affair is Over!

Essential reading for any woman involved with a married man

Nanette Miner, Ed.D. and Sandi Terri
BVC Publishing, Bristol CT
USA

∾

This Affair is Over!

Essential reading for any woman
involved with a married man

By: *Nanette Miner, Ed.D. and Sandi Terri*
Cover Design: Red Barn Studios

Published by: **BVC Publishing, LLC**
P.O. Box 1819
Bristol, CT 06011-1819
USA

Copyright © 1996 by BVC Publishing, LLC
Second printing 2005
ISBN 0-9650666-1-4

❧

Dedication

To all women who are seeking a
better life for themselves.

_____

≈

———— *Table of Contents*

~

Acknowledgments

First and foremost, we'd like to thank all of the women who participated in our survey, and especially those who granted us personal interviews. In addition, we'd like to thank Theodore Avery, Janet, Hilary Estey, Jill, Amby Burridge, and Joe Waggoner for their assistance in putting together various aspects of the book.

ॐ

Preface

Our goal, in writing this book, is to help women who are in pain; to end their affairs with married men and to find the strength to go forward with their life. This strength is found, as it so often is, in the company of other women. There are *thousands* of women across the U.S. who are involved in dead-end affairs. We wanted to find out - who are these women turning to? Are they experiencing the same feelings? Is there a commonality in the way these women deal with their affairs? What can we learn from them?

We've written this book for all the women who are *stalled* in their relationship and don't know where to turn. You are reading this book because you are looking for answers. You cannot find those answers within yourself (yet) because your heart and your mind do not agree. Your mind says "leave him," and your heart says, "but I love him." YOU ARE THE ONLY ONE WHO CONTROLS YOUR LIFE! Take control. Don't allow a "part time" person to have "full time" control of your life, emotions, movements, decisions and commitments.

Caution: For many of you, this book will not be easy to read. It will cause you to take a good look at your situation and ask yourself: Am I happy being involved with a married man? A man that may not be around for the holidays or birthdays? A man who is not there when I need him? A man who makes me his *second choice?* A man who leaves my bed after love making - only to go home to another woman...his wife? You must ask yourself: Am I willing to continue in this lifestyle?

Most men having an affair don't comprehend how their actions affect the women involved. No amount of pain and suffering on your part will cause *him* to take action to change. This is such an important concept, we need to repeat it: *Your* pain is not a reason for *him* to change. If you are ready to take action, this book will free you of your lover. Stop wasting valuable time. An affair will change your life, and not always for the better.

In order to write this book we conducted hundreds of surveys and interviews with women all over the country who were, or are still, involved with a married man. Those of you who are contemplating an affair would do well to take the advice of these women who have "been there" and "done that." Every one of them emphatically stated,
Don't do it.

CHAPTER 1
About Affairs….

It ever has been since time began,
And ever will be, till time lose breath,
That love is a mood - no more - to man,
And love to a woman, is life or death.

Ella Wheeler Wilcox
1850-1919

*M*ost extramarital affairs are between married men and single women. Most women are between the ages of 20 and 40 (65%) when their affair starts, while the men are between 30 and 40 years old (78%). A small percentage of men fail to disclose that they are married at the start of the affair. In cases where the woman has later found out that her lover is married, it may be too late. She may already be too emotionally vested in the relationship.

In most instances, involvement in an affair is not usually deliberate. That is to say, most affairs just "happen." The participants are in the right place at the right time. Many affairs evolve from friendships or work situations.

The reasons for involvement take on many forms. Women have cited they were looking for something new and exciting, they were looking to fill a void in

their lives, or they were looking for happiness.
Herein lies a major lesson - many women that are
involved in affairs are looking outside of
themselves for fulfillment. We all know this to be
an impossible task. No one else can fulfill us or
make us happy. It is entirely up to us. It is entirely
up to *you*.

Fully one third of the women interviewed for this
book stated that they became involved because they
were "pursued relentlessly" by the man involved.
Other reasons for involvement include boredom,
"just sex," mutual attraction and conquest.

Her story:
Debra was involved with Frank for two and a half
years. They were friends for two years prior to any
romantic involvement and Debra knew from the
start that Frank had been married for over 10 years.
Frank began to aggressively pursue her during a
particularly vulnerable period in her life. Debra had
recently discovered that her boyfriend was cheating
on her. She was stunned and saddened by the lack
of fidelity demonstrated by her boyfriend, and
Frank was a willing ear and comforting presence.
Frank's agreement with Debra's assertions that
"men cannot be trusted," and "men are only after
one thing," made Debra *believe* that Frank found
the boyfriend's behavior appalling too. The more
Frank comforted her, the more Debra came to trust
him and have romantic feelings for him. One night
they met for drinks after work. Frank said he was
concerned about her ability to drive and offered to

drive her home. They made love in Debra's living room and he stayed until two in the morning. Debra assured herself that the first time they slept together was purely by accident. Debra certainly did not set out to become romantically involved with Frank.

The next day, Frank called to see how Debra was feeling and to tell her what a wonderful time he had had with her. When she stated that she felt what they had done was wrong, he assured her that his relationship with his wife was purely a convenience for the children's sake, and that she should not have any feelings of remorse since he did not. So began a two and a half year affair. Their affair has now been over for three years, but the pain and anger resurfaces for Debra from time to time. In retrospect she feels that his relentless pursuit overpowered her judgment and that perhaps he had had the outcome planned from the beginning. Although, at the time of their affair, Frank made her feel as though she was the one good thing in his life, she knows that he was not faithful to her during their affair and that he had other affairs before and after theirs. In fact, Frank finally ended the affair by telling her that there was someone else. In 40% of the relationships studied for this book, the man ended the affair. Some of the reasons the men cited were: the wife found out, he found someone else, or, when given an ultimatum by his lover, he couldn't leave his wife.
Debra's words of advice are these: If you are going to become involved with a married man, know what you are getting in to. Don't expect him to be

faithful (if he's having an affair with you, faithfulness is probably not in his vocabulary), don't expect him to leave his wife, know that it (the relationship) is going to end eventually.

Debra's case is similar to that of many women. Her relationship with Frank began as a friendship, but grew to something more during a time when Debra's self-esteem was at a low. Debra generally respected the institution of marriage and would never have planned to enter into a relationship with a man that was married. The fact that Frank countered her fears by assuring her that his marriage was simply a convenience, enabled Debra to rationalize her involvement with him. Frank never once told her that he would leave his wife. Although at times she wished that he would commit more fully to her, Debra knew that Frank was *content*. A wife at home for the children and the "image" he needed to maintain for work, and a girlfriend for fun times and sexual pleasure.

Frank's contentment is a typical state for married men involved in affairs. Although they will tell their lovers that their home life is unbearable and they would leave their wife "if only they could," in fact most men would describe their marriages as happy, although lacking in a particular area such as sexual fulfillment, excitement, or passion. Most men involved in extramarital affairs are not looking for something "better," they are merely looking for something "different." A girlfriend is just the right amount of different that they need.

———————

Debra was lucky in that her lover was always honest about his level of commitment to her and never made her promises which he did not intend to keep.

Her story:

Christiana was not as lucky. Christiana was recently married and had no intention of ever having an affair. She worked in the same office with Walter and his fiancée Joyce. Walter was quite successful and well respected within the company. Christiana and her husband Tim frequently spent time with Joyce and Walter at company functions or couple's get-togethers. Walter was known as a flirt, and loved to "make passes" at the women in the office. One evening when Christiana was working late, Walter returned to the office with a bottle of scotch. They drank the entire bottle, and then went out for drinks when it was gone. They next day he called and told her how much he enjoyed spending the evening with her, and that he couldn't wait to see her again. Christiana saw no problem with this casual association, although she was tremendously attracted to him. After two months of seeing each other on a weekly basis, and daily calls, he professed his love to her and offered to call off his wedding to Joyce, if Christiana said that was what she wanted. She told him no because she didn't really believe that he meant it, and she was happily married at the time. Shortly after, Joyce asked Christiana to be a bridesmaid in her wedding. Christiana agreed, and began to re-think what she was doing with Walter. She told Walter she was uncomfortable and they would have to stop seeing each other.

The wedding took place, all was quiet for awhile, and the two couples continued to see each other on a social basis. One month after the wedding, Christiana and Tim were attending a party at Walter and Joyce's house. As Christiana was leaving an upstairs bathroom, Walter met her outside the door, pushed her inside, closed the door behind them and forcefully kissed her. Although Christiana was stunned, she admits she did not resist. Three months after that encounter, they slept together for the first time. It had been 11 months since they first started seeing each other. Christiana felt that although it was almost a year before the two slept together, she and Walter were still having an "affair." Altogether, Christiana called off their affair eight times, each time vowing to never see him again. Each time Walter wooed her back with promises he'd leave his wife.

By the time Christiana told him the final good-bye, she and Walter had been seeing each other for four years, during which time he promised her at least six times that he would leave his wife and asked her to be patient. She believed him each time. Meanwhile, Christiana's marriage to Tim had ended. She maintains he never knew of the affair. She does however, feel that her involvement with Walter made her look for faults in her husband. Walter is still married, even though Joyce knew of the affair. They now have two children. Joyce, like many wives, chose not to confront Walter or Christiana.

Although Christiana admits to still being consumed by pain over the ending of the affair, she has come to accept it is for the best. With distance and time, it became obvious to Christiana that Walter has no respect for his wife, and no respect for her either. She also feels that Walter will never really leave his wife. A decade after the start of their affair, Walter leaves the occasional voice mail message and checks on her by contacting her friends.

Christiana entered therapy to deal with the pain of both the ending of her marriage and the affair. She focused her energies on her work and enjoyed success that she had not had for nearly the last two years of the affair, while her mind was preoccupied with her relationship with Walter. She sums up her relationship with Walter by saying, "It was full of deceit and lies and I couldn't stand living a double life. I wanted to be with Walter, he was my first choice, but I was his *second* choice. He always told me he was waiting for his wife to divorce him. It was bad enough he couldn't make a decision, but I couldn't wait around for *her* to make a decision (about my life)."

Many of the women interviewed for this book shared stories similar to Christiana's. The men in their lives made promises about "their future" and asked for their lover's patience and understanding of their "situation." Christiana's lover strung her along - as many lovers do - promising her things he knew she wanted to hear, but that he did not intend to deliver. While the men who make these promises may believe they are making their lover feel better, their actions speak louder than their words. And in most cases it is *inaction* that tells the lover exactly where she stands.

Christiana's many efforts to end the affair are not uncommon. Affairs that continue for two or more years typically require five or more attempts at ending the affair before it is finally over. This should be a source of encouragement. The "failure" you perceive in not being able to end it, is simply a part of the process. Christiana is representative of the women that took the initiative to end their affairs. At some point, these women had had enough. They were tired of the lies, no longer believed him when he said he'd leave his wife (of the 53% of men who told their girlfriends they would leave their wives - less than 1% actually did), and, in general, the women were tired of feeling used. One phrase heard over and over was that the women felt they "had wasted too much time" on the relationship.

Her story:

Brenda was involved with Dan for 17 years. Their affair began when she was 20 and he was 34. Dan responded to a police call to her home when some personal items had been stolen. He admitted to Brenda that he entered into their affair for purely selfish reasons. He had just discovered that his wife was having an affair and he wanted to get back at her. Brenda was coming out of a bad relationship and welcomed the attention he showered on her. She felt sorry for Dan and she wanted to protect him. Dan consistently told her that he couldn't leave his wife until his children were grown. When she offered arguments to this excuse, he bolstered it by saying it would cost him too much money, he was afraid he'd lose his job, he didn't want to hurt his wife, and he was afraid of damaging his reputation. Brenda, in an effort to protect Dan, went so far as to talk with the police chief to ensure that Dan would not lose his job!

Dan's wife found out about their affair during the second month. She, like Joyce, chose to ignore the situation. When the children were grown, she and Dan *did* divorce. However, it was Dan's wife that filed for divorce and left him. Brenda believes that Dan would never have divorced his wife. Six years after the end of his marriage, Brenda described their on-going relationship as an affair, even though she is no longer the "other woman." She believes the word "affair" is the appropriate descriptor since Dan still is not committed to her.

During the course of their 17 year affair Brenda,
had two abortions and attempted suicide once. She
tried to end the affair a half dozen times, each time
he won her back with flowers or candy or jewelry.
What really kept her there however, was his
declaration that he "needed her." Brenda entered
therapy for a year, attempting to deal with her
feelings of anger, anxiety, and loss of self esteem.
Her goals were to stop obsessing over him, stop
talking about him to all her friends, and to get him
out of her life.

Over the course of her affair with Dan, Brenda was
waiting for the fairy tale to come true. She held on
to threads of hope, waiting for him to leave his
wife. For all intents and purposes, her fairy tale has
come true, Dan and his wife have split up; and
yet...it's not the blissful outcome Brenda expected.
She realizes that she was in love with a dream; that
the Dan that she was in love with was largely a part
of her imagination. She has come to accept that the
real Dan is unable to provide her with the happiness
she longs for.

For the most part, women who enter into affairs
with married men do not *believe* they are entering
into an affair. Rather, they believe that they are
entering into a long term relationship. Sixty one
percent of the women who participated in the study
had relationships over a year or more; nearly 25%
of these women were involved for five years or
more. What keeps these women bound to these
men for such an extended period of time? The hope

---

that he will leave his wife for her. The tidbits of hope that are thrown her way, such as: "I wish you were my wife; I found a lot we could build *our* house on; I want *you* to have my children; She doesn't make me feel the way you make me feel."

Believe it or not, in almost all cases, a man engaged in an affair is not having an affair because of *you*, he's having an affair for himself. It's not about you - it's about him. He's having an affair because it fuels *his* needs. If you weren't there, someone else would be.

Her story:
Cindy has been involved in her affair with Brad for six months. He told Cindy he would leave his wife when his son "grows up." The two met at the gym where they both work out. Cindy was involved in a lengthy relationship that wasn't making her happy, and Brad's attention and fun-loving manner was very attractive. They were friends and training partners for nine months prior to any romantic involvement. Brad is adamant that he will not leave his marriage until his son is grown. Cindy is unwilling to wait. She has attempted three times to end this affair. Each time he said and did sweet things that won her back. Cindy is experiencing weight loss, loneliness, anger, depression, distraction, crying bouts, anxiety attacks and a general feeling of being out of control of her own life. She knows that this relationship is not going anywhere but rationalizes that she will stay with Brad until something better comes along. In reality,

Cindy may be unable to see the potential for a new relationship with anyone else, while she is consumed with her relationship with Brad.

We want to stress that none of the women are unwilling victims. They may be victims of poor choices, but they know *exactly* the type of relationship they are in, and are consciously continuing the relationship for one reason or another.

The women interviewed for this book gave one or more of the following reasons for getting involved in their affair. Which of these apply to you?

- ❏ Felt unloved
- ❏ Felt unfulfilled
- ❏ Believed that someone else could fulfill them
- ❏ Believed that someone else could provide them with happiness
- ❏ Lonely
- ❏ Attraction
- ❏ Bored
- ❏ Spent large amounts of time with a "friend" of the opposite sex, discussing intimate feelings that are usually reserved for loved ones (for example: the importance of sex, children, values)
- ❏ Looking for a distraction

☐ Recently divorced

☐ Ran into an old boyfriend

☐ Curious

☐ Conquest

☐ Just looking for sex

☐ Looking for a vague sense of "something different"

☐ Friendship/companionship

☐ To fill a void

☐ Fell in love

☐ Pursued relentlessly by the married man

Chapter 2
If You Try Hard Enough,
You Can Rationalize Anything

"Autobiography in 5 short chapters"

Chapter 1: I walk down the street. There is a deep hole in the sidewalk. I fall in. I am lost. I am helpless. It isn't my fault. It takes forever to find the way out.

Chapter 2: I walk down the same street. There is a deep hole in the sidewalk. I pretend I don't see it. I fall in again. I can't believe I'm in the same place, but...it isn't my fault. It still takes a long time to get out.

Chapter 3: I walk down the same street. There is a deep hole in the sidewalk. I see it is there. I still fall in. It's a habit. Yet..my eyes are open, I know where I am. It is my fault. I get out immediately.

Chapter 4: I walk down the same street. There is a deep hole in the sidewalk. I walk around it.

Chapter 5: I walk down another street.

Portia Nelson

*I*n the previous chapter you were introduced to women that represented different affair-scenarios: long-term, short-term, still involved, no longer involved, etc. No matter what the individual situation is, there seems to be a commonality around extramarital affairs which involves the lines/excuses that your loved one "feeds" you. The lines that you hear involve when he'll leave his spouse, or the conditions under which he'll leave his spouse.

The men involved in our case studies were nearly equally split regarding their honesty about whether or not they would leave their wives. Fifty three percent promised that they would, while 45% never made any promises. Following are listed some of the conditions under which the men said they would leave their wives. Which have you heard?

After…
☐ The baby is born
☐ My son/daughter turns 18
☐ My son/daughter moves out
☐ My child graduates
☐ We close (he and wife) on our new house
☐ My loan is paid off
☐ The holidays are over
☐ Fall/winter/spring/summer is over
☐ Our vacation (he and wife)
☐ I've saved "x" amount of money
☐ My wife files for divorce

Let's examine a few of these situations for validity.

"I'll leave after the holidays are over." Presumably he doesn't want to ruin the holidays for his family.

What about you? Doesn't he care that you'll be
sitting home alone during the holidays, missing him
and wishing he were there?

"I'll leave after our vacation is over." Does he
intend to show his family one last time how much
he cares, and then come home and dump them?
How will a week on the beach, or in the mountains,
give him peace of mind?

"I'll leave after the baby is born." A misguided
sense of loyalty is at work here. Does he really
believe his wife will be grateful that he waited until
after she had their baby before leaving her?

"I'll leave when I've saved "x" amount of money,"
or "when my loan is paid off."   What do money
and love have to do with one another? How will
having money saved make the split any easier for
him/his wife/you? Plenty of people are deeply in
love and deeply in debt.

"I'll leave her if *you* tell me to." A classic case of
not taking responsibility for one's own actions. In
this case he's able to blame you should anything go
wrong, and he'll forever be able to get what he
wants from you by invoking "look what I did for
you." Are you willing to take responsibility for his
relationship with his wife *and* his relationship with
you?

Of those men that said they would not leave their
wives, the following excuses were given:

- ☐ She won't give me a divorce
- ☐ I told her I wanted a divorce, but she cried
- ☐ It will cost too much money (alimony, child support)
- ☐ My family/her family
- ☐ I'm afraid she'll commit suicide
- ☐ I'll lose my job
- ☐ Too many people will get hurt
- ☐ I don't want to hurt her
- ☐ Health (his/hers/parents/etc.)
- ☐ My reputation will be ruined
- ☐ My in-laws paid for....
- ☐ The children
- ☐ My religion
- ☐ The age difference between us (you and he) is too great - eventually you'll leave me

Let's examine a few of these excuses for validity.

"I told her I wanted a divorce, but she cried." We'll combine this with," I don't want to hurt her." What about you? You cry a lot. Why is he more willing to hurt you than hurt his wife? What does this say about the way in which he values your relationship with him?

"It will cost too much money." Kings have been known to abdicate the throne for the woman they love.

"I can't leave because of my/her/parents health." Walter told Christiana that he had a bad heart, and the stress of ending his marriage could prove fatal for him! This is a classic guilt trip. He's got you so worried that if someone dies it will be *your* fault (in a convoluted way), how could you possibly deal with the guilt the rest of your life?

"My reputation will be ruined." Very few men hide the fact that they are having an affair from their buddies and co-workers. Girlfriends are seen as trophies to be paraded before the admiring group. Frequently the wife also knows about the affair. Brenda stated that "the whole town knew" of her affair with Brad. What reputation is he referring to? Is he implying that it's OK to cheat, but it's not OK to be divorced? And what about *your* reputation?

The most valid excuse that a man will offer is that he cannot leave because of his children. While there are men that leave their homes and children everyday, some men cannot and will not do it. Again, this may only be an excuse, but it will be difficult for you to determine if he is sincerely committed to his children's welfare, or if it is the excuse he is using because he knows it is the only one which you will accept as valid.

It is true that when you step back and examine these lines objectively, they are absurd. And yet, seemingly, women continue to fall for them again and again. Part of this stems from the fact that we naturally believe what our loved ones tell us - why would they lie to us? And part of the believing is due to the fact that we are desperate to believe that the relationship is going somewhere.

In some cases, your lover is telling you exactly where you stand, or exactly how he feels about your relationship, and yet you refuse to hear it. Walter told Christiana, "If you really knew me, you'd hate me." What Christiana heard was "my wife is turning me into a person I can't stand." Christiana heard this as a call for help. It made her love him more. It made her want to "save" him from his unhappy marriage. In actuality what Walter was probably saying was the absolute truth - that he treated women poorly, and he knew it.

In many cases, and all types of situations, we hear what we want to hear. Have you ever experienced the phenomena of buying a new car, and then seeing fifty *just like it* that you never noticed before? This is selective awareness. When your lover is telling you one thing, but you are hearing another, this is selective hearing.

Her Story:
Tammy has been involved with Billy for one and a half years. Billy is married with two children, and recently bought a new home with his wife. Tammy and Billy work together on the third shift and frequently spend their mornings or afternoons together with their children (Tammy has one child), while Billy's wife is at work. What began as a friendship between two people with mutual interests and compatible schedules has become a passionate

love affair. Tammy has asked Billy for more of a commitment. Billy's response was, "I can't live without you. Don't ask me to choose between my wife and you." What Tammy heard was, "You're the most important thing in my life and making me choose will cause me pain." In actuality, what Billy is saying is, "Don't make me choose, or *you* will be hurt. I will choose to stay in my marriage." Tammy didn't force Billy to choose.

Brenda purchased a new waterbed. The first time that Dan slept in it with her he said, "I can't believe how comfortable this is. I can't wait to get one of these." What Brenda heard was, "I can't wait to move in and share this bed with you." It's probably safe to assume that what Dan was really saying was, "I'll have to go out and buy one like this."

It's very difficult to remain objective when our hearts are involved in our decision making. Many times we know the reality of our situation, but we choose not to acknowledge it. Although many women expressed that they felt "duped" or "used" by their lover, the responsibility does not lie entirely with the man. Many times the man is telling you exactly how he feels, and exactly what role you play in his life. However, you have heard something different. You must have the courage to stand back and assess the situation for what it really is.

Take a few moments now to ask yourself: Do I believe my lover will leave his wife? Do I believe he will leave her for *me*?

When asked if they truly believed their lover would leave his wife, 41% of our survey respondents said "No" while 1% said "Yes, *but not for me.*"

_____

Chapter 3
All Right,
Sometimes These Things Do Work Out

There's a difference between interest and
commitment.
When you're interested in doing something, you do
it only when it's convenient.
When you're committed to something, you accept
no excuses; only results.

Ken Blanchard

ou'll notice that this chapter is
short in comparison to the others.
There is good reason for this.
Most affairs do not end blissfully,
with the man and girlfriend together. Of our survey
respondents, *less than one percent* of the men left
their wives for their girlfriends - although nearly
53% said that they would leave. In some instances,
the man did leave his wife, and yet *still* did not
commit to his girlfriend. As stated in the preface,
this book is not intended to discourage you, but
rather *encourage* you. If you are wondering if your
affair will ever turn into something more, keep
reading. Gauge your lover's actions against those
men that have taken steps toward a life with their
lover.

Her story:
Caitlin and Michael met at work. Initially Caitlin
wasn't at all interested in Michael. After they were
first introduced, he called her a few times to ask her
out for drinks. She refused him each time. As she
got to know him better however, she began to feel
that Michael was "everything my husband was not."
Caitlin had been married for three years, but admits
to having doubts about long term compatibility with
her husband, even before their marriage.

When Caitlin and Michael finally did make love,
two months after they had started seeing each other
for drinks or dinner on a regular basis, Caitlin felt
that there "was more to us than just that moment."
Being with Michael became Caitlin's sole focus.
They talked on the phone constantly, and got
together every chance they could. Each time they
were together, it was harder to say good-bye.

Although Caitlin felt that she wanted more of a
relationship - and more of a commitment - with
Michael, she believed it was unrealistic since they
were both married and neither one was comfortable
with the idea of divorce. However, three months
into their affair, Michael told her that he couldn't
take it anymore, that no matter what happened, he
could no longer live a "half-life." He drew up a
separation agreement with his wife and got an
apartment of his own.

Although Caitlin was thrilled, there was now the
added pressure that she, too, should do something

---

about the marriage she was in. It took a few months longer, but Caitlin also got an apartment of her own. Caitlin stresses that although she and Michael wanted to be together every minute, they purposely avoided living together so that they had the time and space to sort through their personal lives.

Their affair lasted for nine months, during which time each separated, and then divorced their respective spouses. It was not an easy time for either of them. Caitlin stated that leaving her husband to start a life with Michael, "was the most difficult thing I have ever done, but, it was worthwhile in order to not be trapped in a marriage that was unfulfilling."

Caitlin and Michael have been together for sixteen years, have been married for thirteen, and have two daughters ages nine and eleven. Although Caitlin and Michael now have a happy life together, Caitlin cautions other women to look closely for signs that your affair is *more* than an affair - "look for signs of commitment and action from your lover. When Michael told me he wanted to divorce his wife, and then moved out of the home he shared with her shortly thereafter, I knew that I was more than an affair to him. I knew that he was willing to make a commitment to *my* happiness, as well as his own."

Look for these signs of commitment from your lover:

☐ He offers no excuses about why he cannot leave (alimony, child support, mortgage, in-laws)
☐ He and his wife begin sleeping in separate rooms
☐ He moves out of his home with his wife
☐ He leaves his wife within one year of starting the affair
☐ He is willing to "give everything up" - home, reputation - and *does* so
☐ He considers what's best for you, or what's best for both of you, not just what is best for him
☐ He doesn't move in to your place and doesn't *assume* he can (he's not looking to you for support). He has the strength to make his own choices and do what's best for him
☐ He files for separation
☐ He files for divorce

Her Story:
Tracy and Bob have been married for two years. They have one child together. At the time of the start of their affair, Bob had been married for nine months. They met at a bar and were instantly attracted to one another. Although at first Bob did not let Tracy know that he was married, he admitted it on their fifth date. Tracy felt that being a "mistress" would be unacceptable and told Bob the relationship was over. They parted as friends, but

Bob frequently called and asked her out, telling her
that "she was the one for him." Tracy still
continued to refuse. Seven months after they
stopped seeing each other, Bob left his wife and
moved into his own apartment. He called Tracy
and asked to meet her for dinner - he had something
important to tell her. She refused. He then asked
her over to *his place* for dinner. He had indeed
been serious when he said that he was unhappy in
his marriage and that he wanted to be with her.
They dated for two years before marrying. Tracy is
comfortable that their marriage is grounded in
reality and not a romantic illusion.

Not all affairs end in marriage; yet the parties
involved can still be content with the relationship.
Not all women want a commitment of marriage
from their lovers, and not all men are so unhappy at
home that they are willing to give up their marriage.
When two individuals with this way of thinking
meet, they can have a long-term and fulfilling
affair.

Her Story:
Lois and Ted have been involved for four years. He
is 20 years older than she and had been married
eight years at the time that they met. Ted has never
told her that he will leave his wife, and Lois doesn't
really want him to. Lois and Ted have two children
together. Ted visits every evening with Lois and
the children; he supports them financially and also
pays for Lois' college tuition. Lois has never
attempted to end the affair. She maintains that she

is happy with her relationship with Ted, but admits that "eventually" she will probably outgrow him and leave him. While she is not unhappy, Lois wants to caution other women, "Don't do it. I love Ted, but I would never get involved with a married man again."

Her Story:
Ginny, a woman nearing 50, and Al, have been sporadically involved for eight and a half years. Ginny is widowed and Al has been married for almost thirty years. Ginny began in the affair because she was looking for a friend and companion. She is extremely content in the relationship. She makes no demands of him, and likewise, he makes no demands of her. She is able to come and go as she pleases, without having to "answer" to anyone. Al has never promised her that he would leave his wife and she has never asked him to. Ginny stated that they both agree that if Al were to leave, it would cost him too much money. They each cite this reason as an explanation for the fact that the topic of further commitment between them is never brought up. Ginny and Al have each found the degree of fulfillment that they are looking for in the affair. Ginny is representative of one-half of a percent of the women surveyed. These women are not looking for anything more meaningful than a part-time relationship with a married man.

While there are always exceptions to the rule, the vast majority of extramarital affairs cause pain, anguish, despair and a loss of self-esteem and self-respect. Chapter four will tell you more about the reality of extramarital affairs.

———————

Chapter 4
The Reality of Dead-End Affairs

That which does not kill you,
makes you stronger

Author Unknown

*T*his chapter must be read with an open mind. You will need to take a look at yourself and your relationship with a critical eye. It's time to evaluate your relationship - is it going anywhere? Do you want it to?

The women interviewed for this book used the following words to describe their emotions during their affairs: desperation, loneliness, loss of self esteem, anger, jealousy, depression, anxiety, betrayal, suicidal thoughts, distraction, bouts of crying, loss of control, vulnerability; in addition to citing physical symptoms such as weight loss and health problems and addictions such as drinking, drugs, smoking, eating or shopping. (There are self help books regarding addictions, obsessive and compulsive behaviors that should be utilized, if you find this pertains to you. We recommend a few books in the Suggested Readings section.)

Life with a married man, while he stays married, will always include pain. But, in a life without him, the pain will eventually dissipate. Which would you prefer?

As stated earlier, most affairs are not planned in advance, they just "happen." Most women who involve themselves with married men, enter into the affair believing that they will maintain control, that they will enter into it just to see "what it's like," or that they will be able to maintain emotional distance from this man. The reality is that once you have slept with him, you are "hooked." You may not be hooked in an addictive sort of way, but you *are* hooked in that you have stepped over the emotional boundary you had once had to protect yourself. Why does this happen? The primary reason is that women equate love-making with *love*, while men equate love-making with...sex. Sex is an act that most men are able to enter into without a lot of emotional baggage. Conversely, most women view sexual involvement as an extremely emotional experience which is fraught with undertones of commitment and promise, whether these words are actually spoken or not.

What is the most jarring realization for women - and the most difficult fact to accept - is that 99% of the married men having affairs are not having an affair because of *you*. They are having the affair for themselves. The affair fills some void or psychological need that they are trying to compensate for. In order to keep you with them, they tell you that you are able to fulfill that part of them that is missing. However, the reality is that if it were not you, it would be someone else. This is substantiated by the fact that most men involved in extramarital affairs have been involved in more than one. As we stated earlier, a woman will not find fulfillment with a married man - with any man - if she is relying on someone else to fulfill her. The same is true of your married lover. If he is running from something, *to you*, he is not working toward finding happiness within himself. *You cannot provide it for him.*

Affairs are based on deception, and deception is difficult to sustain. The most obvious deception involves you and your lover's wife. On the one hand, your lover has most likely kept his affair with you a secret from his spouse. In many cases where the spouse does know, she chooses to overlook it. On the other hand, your lover has probably told you that his wife is the "bad guy" - she hates sex, they haven't slept together in months/years, she's indifferent to his needs, and so on.

Her Story:
Amy and Brian were lovers for three years. Amy finally came to the realization that Brian was not going to leave his wife, and told Brian that their affair was over. A few weeks later, Amy and Brian were attending the same party, given by Amy's friend. Brian had been telling the friend how much he missed Amy and the friend thought she would attempt to bring them back together. At the end of the evening, Brian drove Amy home and asked to come into her apartment to play her a song that he

had recorded especially for her. As the song was playing, he told her how much he missed her, that he had not slept with his wife in over two months, and that he was taking steps to end his marriage in order to be with her. He told her he wanted desperately to make love to her. Amy told him no, it was over. When Amy opened the door for Brian to leave, she found his wife standing on her doorstep. A confrontation ensued. Amy assured his wife that the affair was over between them and that Brian was there, that evening, in an attempt to seduce her since he had not slept with his wife in two months. Brian's wife revealed that they had had sex that morning!

The married man involved in an affair is enmeshed in a life of duplicity, deceit and lies. Can you live with a person of this nature? Before you answer, ask yourself these questions: Do you trust your lover? Do you believe your lover is having another affair, or would have another affair if the right circumstances arose? Has your lover had other affairs? If you were to marry your lover, are you comfortable in the belief that he would be committed solely to you?

When asked to honestly answer these questions, most survey respondents stated that they felt "duped" by their lovers, and that they believed their lovers have had, or would have, other affairs, if the opportunity arose. One respondent summed up the end of her relationship with her lover this way "I eventually realized that I have no respect for a cheater."

During the Affair
❧

Let's take a deeper look into the words that women use to describe their emotions while they are involved in an affair.

Desperation - Christiana stated she felt desperation in her relationship with Walter because she wanted so badly to begin a life with him and have his children. Until she had met Walter, Christiana hadn't really thought about having children. The time just didn't seem right to her. But, after a year with Walter, she felt that they were soul mates and because she felt so close to him, she wanted to bear his children. At first, Walter told her that he didn't want any children. Then, as Christiana continued to bring up the subject, he said that he certainly didn't want to have them with his wife, but *if* he ever did want children, it would be with Christiana. Christina took this as a commitment that they would have a family together. In retrospect Christiana realizes that Walter never committed to having children with her. The most he had ever committed to was saying that *if there came a time* when he would want them, he'd want them with her. When Christiana was told by her gynecologist that if she ever intended to have children, she should start soon due to potential medical problems, Christiana began to have feelings of desperation about her relationship with Walter. When would he leave his wife? When could they begin their life? How many years before she could have his child? What if was too late? Why wouldn't he leave his wife for her, knowing how badly she wanted his child and knowing that time was running out for her? She admits, "I lost so many night's sleep consumed with thoughts about why he wasn't as committed to our relationship, and having a family, as I was."

"I thought I could win him over with great sex," she continued. "I believed that if our love making were 100% better than the sex he had with his wife, it would only be natural that he would leave her for me. I was so desperate to make each of our encounters better than the last - more imaginative, longer, more exotic - he would see how desperately I loved him, and he would naturally love me that much in return."

Loss of Self Esteem - Linda and Jim have been involved for two and a half years. Linda feels that she's given all of her "self" to Jim, and has gotten little in return. Over the course of their affair she has given up - or lost - most of her friends, and has no social life outside of her get-togethers with Jim. Linda's relationship with Jim depends on Jim's availability. Jim's wife attends a cooking class every Wednesday night. Therefore, Wednesdays are Jim and Linda's night together for sure. However, sometimes Jim's wife will go out with her friends, or baby-sit for her sister's children in another town on Friday or Saturday night. Jim doesn't usually know until that day whether or not his wife will be home in the evening, so Linda keeps those evenings free *in case* Jim's wife goes out and *in case* Jim calls her to tell her he's free.

Sometimes Jim and Linda will make plans to go to dinner or catch a movie, and at the last minute he'll have to cancel because his wife made plans for them that he wasn't aware of. "I'm always expected to re-arrange my schedule to fit his situation," she stated. "My friends have given up on me. Even when I do make plans with my friends, I might cancel them at the last minute to be with Jim. They don't want to be treated like second class citizens, and, I finally realized, neither do I."

Once, Linda ran out of gas on her way home from work. It was about 5:30 in the evening and raining. She called Jim for help from her cell phone. He said to her, "You know I'd help you if I could, but I have to get home and change, we're going to a dinner party tonight."

"At the time I said, 'That's OK, I understand', and I called my emergency road-side service for help," Linda related. "Now, I look back and think, 'What am I? An idiot? A dinner party was more important than me being stranded at the side of the road? Why couldn't he come help me and give *his wife* some excuse?' I'm settling for whatever I can get, and I ask myself, 'Why?'. If Jim were a single guy, there's no way I'd stand for this kind of treatment. One date canceled at the last minute, I might tolerate, but two or three? I'd never let a single guy treat me this way. I let Jim get away with a lot because of his "situation," somehow I think it's a legitimate excuse. But really, why should I tolerate such rude behavior?"

Suicidal Thoughts - Brenda admits she tried to kill herself once in the 17 years she's been involved with Dan. "I was just so miserable," she says, "I couldn't understand why he wouldn't leave his wife for me. I would do it for him, if the situation was reversed. I kept comparing myself to his wife, wasn't I prettier? Didn't I treat him better? He always told me I did. I guess I was in so much pain, I wanted him to be in pain too. I couldn't make him do what I wanted, but I could control what happened to me, and in a crazy way, make him pay for the pain that I was in."

Loneliness - "I realize that I'm not in a real relationship during those times when I should be happiest," stated Lois. "When I get an A in school, I want to share it with Ted, but I can't always call him when I want to. At Christmas time, and other holidays, I try to make the children wait until he comes over before we celebrate, but it's getting harder as they get older. I'm really busy during the day with the kids and school, and Ted is really good about being here in the evenings, so most of the time I don't feel lonely until late at night, or, like I said, during times when I want to share something good or happy with Ted, and he's not there for me."

Bouts of Crying - Virtually every woman surveyed stated that she cried, or was near tears, a large percentage of the time. "It's a combination of loneliness, desperation, feeling dejected and unlovable. It's all sorts of feelings that you don't know how to express, or overcome, and you just end up crying," says Brenda.

Christiana says, "I cried because I couldn't tell the difference between the truth and the lies. He would tell me he couldn't take it any more, and he was leaving her, and then three or four weeks would go by and he wouldn't bring it up again. I cried because I felt I had no control over what was happening. He had all the control in the relationship. In some ways he still does. I cried because I was extremely depressed. I was obsessed with him and what he was doing - was he making love to her? Were they out to dinner together? I cried every time they went on vacation".

"I cry now because I'm sad that I believed him for so long and lost sight of myself. I cry because I'm still in love with him, but I've accepted the fact that he'll never leave for me, or because of me. I cry now mostly because I feel sorry for myself. That's why I started therapy, I couldn't stand the crying, I couldn't stand the hopelessness. That's the thing. I felt hopeless."

Betrayal - The incidents of betrayal cited by the women surveyed run the gamut from contracting a venereal disease from the lover, to finding out the lover had gotten another woman pregnant - and left his wife for the pregnant woman, to losing the lover to *another* lover. Some cases of betrayal might be considered extreme and some might be considered trivial, but they are all significant to the woman who is experiencing them. One lover took his girlfriend to dinner to tell her he had asked his wife for divorce. She was thrilled. Her mind raced, imagining all the wonderful times they would soon have together. The lover then announced that his wife had said no, and so he wouldn't be getting divorced after all.

Jealousy - "Jealousy is a bad emotion," stated Tracy, "it's probably the worst emotion. I was jealous of his wife. I know that sounds crazy, she should have been the one jealous of me, but I felt that she was *my* rival in every way."

Christiana said, "I was jealous when I found out what he bought her for Christmas or her birthday. Twice, when I had bought something for myself - skis and golf clubs - he went out and bought those things for *her*. I love sports, and so does he, but instead of enjoying those things with me, he wanted *her* to get involved in them. Aside from the big things, like presents and vacations, I was even jealous that they would wake up in the morning and have a cup of coffee together."

Brenda stated, "I couldn't stand the jealousy I felt when he would leave my bed to go home to her. The pain was unbelievable."

————————

In Retrospect
◈

"I was afraid to break it off with him, because I was afraid there was no man that could compare to him, or that I would never have the same feelings for another man," said Christiana. "I know now that that was all in my head. I know that I'm not special to him - I'm just another woman. My affair caused me *a lot* of pain. I'm still in a lot of pain, *years* later. But, I think pain can bring about growth. I know it won't be easy to get over him, but I know that I *have* to do it."

Ginny, who is happy with the level of involvement in her affair with Al, stated, "These women have to realize that a married man *cannot* commit to you. If they are comfortable with that thought, they can continue on in their affair. If they can't handle that thought, then they need to find a man that can commit."

Debra admits, "I'm not proud of what I did. I would never do it again. Put yourself in the wife's position. What would you think about a mistress? You'd think she was a tramp. I'm not a tramp. I have more respect for myself than that. I'm glad our affair is over. When I get married, I hope my husband never cheats on me."

"I think my biggest mistake during my affair with Dan, was believing that if he left his wife and came to me, all his problems would be solved. And, I couldn't understand why he didn't see that too," said Brenda. "He was so miserable with his wife, and I could have made him so happy, yet he wouldn't leave her. *I* was the one who didn't see the reality of the circumstances. I used to ask him, 'what have you got to lose?' Now that I've got perspective on the whole situation, I understand he had *everything* to lose. His home, his children in some ways, probably a lot of money, perhaps his family - no one in his family had ever been divorced. Dan knew better. Dan knew he would lose *a lot* by coming to me. He wasn't blinded by our love, but I was! I know now that what was most important to him wasn't our love, but maintaining his lifestyle. He didn't want to rock the boat. And as long as I was content, so to speak, to remain his girlfriend, he had no need to change the situation."

After the Affair
~

The reasons women gave for ending their affairs were many, and varied. Some common themes emerged, such as, "guilt; tired of the lies (telling them or being the recipient of them); I lost respect for him/myself; I realized he'd never leave his wife;" and, "I deserved more/better."

Many women involved with married men are eventually dumped by them. Some of the reasons the men left were: they found another lover, their wives found out and gave them an ultimatum - the man chose the wife, the girlfriend gave him an ultimatum - and he chose the wife, and one man who realized he was making a mistake and said, "I don't know why I started this. I must be crazy."

In some cases, the parting is mutual. Each party realizes they are not getting the fulfillment they desire, and they choose to end an affair that is going nowhere.

It didn't matter whether the affair had been over for six months or 10 years, the emotions expressed by the women were similar when asked how they felt now that the affair was over. Immediately following the end of the affair, many said that they were angry and resentful; but stressed that anger can be good in that it can be motivating, and in many cases the anger they felt helped them to maintain their determination not to return to the

affair. Many expressed relief and acceptance, and a
few said that, after a time, they were happy it was
over.

Of those women involved in affairs that lasted a
year or more, all said that they felt they had wasted
too much time. Those women that entered into the
affair because they were pursued by the man,
expressed sentiments of being used or duped.

Observations and Conclusions
✍

Men who are involved in extramarital affairs all
share one characteristic. They are liars. They lie to
their wives, they lie to themselves and believe it or
not, they even lie to you. When you attempt to end
your relationship, you will hear all sort of lines
intended to win you over. Your lover will say
whatever he thinks you need to hear - "My wife and
I don't sleep together; I've never loved anyone the
way I love you; I've never made love to any woman
the way we make love; I've never cheated on my
wife before; I've spoken with an attorney; Look at
all I've done for you," and so on. Interestingly, if
your lover cannot win you over with guilt - "I'll be
ruined financially; My family will disown me" -
he'll switch to pity - "My wife has cancer and I
can't leave her (the girlfriend later found out his
wife never had cancer); You don't understand how
hard it is for me; I can't go on without you; Life
with my wife is intolerable." All of these *lines* are a

diversion in hopes of keeping you with him. They are words of desperation. He will say virtually anything in order to have his cake and eat it too.

If you are involved with a married man, remember this: he is not committing to his wife, nor is he committing to you. Stop enabling him. Stop reinforcing his behavior by staying with him or taking him back after an attempt at ending the relationship. Don't be desperate for this man's love. Do not settle for the worst you can tolerate.

Actions speak louder than words. Yes, this is a cliché, but think about the implications. What is your lover doing to improve your situation? Is he sleeping in a separate room? Has he seen an attorney? Has he filed for divorce? Has he moved out of his home with his wife? Has he told you he's done these things, or do you know them to be true? Is he making plans for a future with you? Less than 1% of the survey respondent's lovers actually left their wives to be with their lovers. In other words, **99% never took action**. In all the cases where the man and girlfriend ended up together, the man took action to end his marriage in under one year.

You cannot control your lover or his actions. You cannot change him, nor expect him to change *for you*. Trying harder to please him will not work. If he is truly miserable in his marriage, he will take action to change his life. At some level your lover is content with the way things are. Contented people are not motivated to make a change in their life. Although the situation may seem intolerable to you, if your lover is not working toward a change in his circumstances, he is content with the status-quo.

Is your relationship based on fact or fantasy? If you are motivated to regain control of your life, Chapter 5 will provide you with positive actions to take.

Chapter 5
Getting Your Life Back in Order

You gain strength, courage and confidence by every experience in which you stop to look fear in the face.

You are able to say to yourself, "I've lived through this horror, I can take the next thing that comes along."

You must do the thing you think you cannot do.

Eleanor Roosevelt

Are you:

- ☐ Fed-up with being alone on the holidays?
- ☐ Tired of having a broken heart?
- ☐ Tired of broken promises? Canceled dates?
- ☐ Fed up with the lies and deceit?
- ☐ Tired of being a convenience?
- ☐ Drained by blow-after-blow to your self-esteem?
- ☐ Discontented with being his *second choice*?
- ☐ Tired of the emptiness inside you?
- ☐ Ready to make a change?

Then it's time for <u>you</u> to take action.
To go on with your life without your lover is going
to be one of the hardest things you've ever had to
do. But, if you desire a happier, fuller. life this is
what you *must* do. If you've decided to end your
affair, set a date to do it and prepare for it. Start
now by making a commitment to yourself.

On the next page you will find a list of 10 steps that
are essential to transforming your life. The page is
purposely set apart from the others so that you can
rip it out and carry it with you. You will find a full
explanation of each step after that.

Ten Steps To Regaining Your Life

1. Accept the fact that he is not leaving.

2. Stop your association with him.

3. Stop obsessing about him.

4. Seek outside help.

5. Start a "new life."

6. Keep a journal.

7. Make a list of goals.

8. Re-establish your friendships.

9. Become spiritual.

10. Fake it 'till you make it.

---

1. Accept the fact that he is not leaving.

Acceptance is the most important step toward starting your new life. If he hasn't done it yet, you can be 99% certain that he will not leave his wife.

2. Stop your association with him.

If you continue to see him you will not be able to think clearly and heal yourself. Distance will give you a better perspective. Stop sleeping with him - this is imperative in order to break those emotional and physical ties. Stop accepting his phone calls. Don't return his messages. Change your number to an unlisted number. Stop calling *him.* Accept no more gifts. Return letters unopened, or throw them out. If you accept financial assistance from him, stop. Move out of his rented apartment, stop taking money from him. Cut people off or walk away when his name comes up in conversation.

3. Stop obsessing about him.

Stop fantasizing. Stop talking to your friends about him. Begin to control your thoughts. Every time you think or dwell on him - stop. Change your thought patterns. When you control your thoughts you automatically begin to control your emotions. Every time you think of him, get up, go to the gym, watch TV, read a book, take a walk. To change your thought pattern will take much practice. Thankfully, you are 100% in control of your thoughts.

---

4. Seek outside help.

Getting outside help means reaching out. This is a necessary step for many women. Seek professional help, such as a therapist, and/or read self-help books (see Suggested Readings), and/or listen to self-help audio tapes in your car or at home. Join a support group or start one.

5. Start a "new life."

Start doing wonderful things for yourself. Pamper yourself - get a facial, massage, manicure, new hair cut. Take a bubble bath. Buy yourself a dozen roses.

Take up a sport. What have you always wanted to do? Try skiing, hiking, scuba diving, roller blading, golf. What a great way to meet new people!

Take a class. Learn a new language, cooking, painting.

Go to a museum, play or concert.

Do volunteer work in your free time. Volunteer at a homeless shelter, a hospital, an AIDS residence. Giving to others less fortunate than yourself will give you a new perspective.

Join a gym. You'll look and feel healthier and it's great for your body, mind, and soul.

Get a dog, cat or other pet. This will certainly keep you busy; plus, they attract other people and they give you something to talk about to new acquaintances.

Take a vacation. Try a vacation spot that caters to singles.

Get involved in your work. Set your sights on a promotion, or enhancing your present position, or apply for a new job.

Move or relocate. You may consider this a drastic measure. Take a look around your home. Are there memories of him everywhere? Would it be easier to leave those memories behind? If you're able to move to a new city - do it! If not, move across town.

All of this is intended to keep your body busy and your mind occupied.

6. Keep a journal.

This is an excellent tool to help you heal from the relationship. In one section, put down all the positive things that you want to do for yourself. In a different section record your negative emotions and the things you hated about the relationship. Read it when you're feeling blue and thinking of calling him. It will remind you about how bad things really were and when you're feeling weak, it will give you strength.

7. *Make a list of goals.*

This should be a list of things you'd like to accomplish - from small to big, and short-term to long-range goals. Don't view this as a "wish list." If you set a goal with no intention of acting on it, then it's merely a wish. Focus on fun and interesting things.

A small goal might be going to a movie by yourself each week or redecorating your bathroom. A big goal might be to get a new job, get a degree, or run the New York Marathon. Make sure your goals are not too easy, or too difficult, make them reasonably obtainable. Reaching your goals will help to reinforce your self-worth. Mixing both large and small goals will allow you to consistently see positive results.

8. *Re-establish your friendships.*

Re-kindle those relationships you let go, or make new friends. Throw a party: a wine-tasting party or a tree-trimming party. Planning a party around the holidays will require you to focus your attention on the party and help to keep your mind off of him.

9. *Become spiritual.*

Spirituality does not necessarily mean going to church, synagogue or other place of worship. Spirituality in this sense means getting in touch with yourself This may include going to religious events, but it may also mean taking up yoga or meditation or getting closer to nature. Commit a certain amount of time each day to enjoying the essence of life.

10. Fake it till you make it.

Keep your head held high. When you're feeling depressed put a smile on your face. Look and act the part of a confident, self-assured woman. Show your family, friends, and your ex-lover that life is great! The more you portray this image, the more you will become it.

None of these steps are easy, but they are necessary. You will have good days and bad days. You may even experience "withdrawal" symptoms. Make sure you have your family and friends there for you, and keep busy. Should you slip and see him or talk with him, acknowledge it as a mistake and go on - don't be hard on yourself. When you learned to walk as a baby, you didn't do it on the first try! You took baby steps until you were balanced and confident enough to do it on your own. The same principle applies here. Rejoice in your small successes. With every passing day you will get stronger.

We wish you well...

SUGGESTED READING AND REFERENCES

Men Who Can't Be Faithful, by Carol Botwin
New York, NY: Warner Books, 1989

How to Fall Out of Love, by Dr. Debora Phillips
with Robert Judd
New York, NY: Warner Books, 1982

Women Who Love too Much, by Robin Norwood
New York, NY: Simon and Schuster, 1986

How to Break Your Addiction to a Person, by
Howard M. Halpern, Ph.D.
New York, NY: Bantam Books, 1983

**Ten Stupid Things Women do to Mess Up Their
Lives,** by Dr. Laura Schlessinger
New York, NY: Harper Collins, 1995

Secret Lovers, by Dr. Luann Linquist
Lexington, MA: Lexington Books, 1989

Love and Addiction, by Stanton Peele
New York, NY: Taplinger, 1975

Your Erroneous Zones, by Dr. Wayne Dyer
New York, NY: Avon Printing, 1977

Don't Call That Man, by Rhonda Findling
Hyperion; November 17, 1999

Affairs: How to deal with extra-marital relationships (A Spectrum book), by Tony Lake
Prentice-Hall; 1981

Love Affairs: Marriage & Infidelity, by Richard Taylor
Prometheus Books; Revised edition March 1, 1997

The Mistress : Histories, Myths and Interpretations of the "Other Woman," by Victoria Griffin
Bloomsbury USA; October 15, 1999

New Other Woman, by Laurel Richardson
Free Press; March 16, 1987

The Single Woman-Married Man Syndrome, by Richard, M.D. Tuch
Rowman & Littlefield Publishers; June 1, 2002

Why I Cheat on My Wife: Confessions of Anonymous Men, by Terrick Wilson
Writers Club Press; December 1, 2001

Never Satisfied: How & Why Men Cheat, by Michael Baisden
Legacy Publishing (GA); July 1, 1995

We'd like to hear from you!

Please write us and let us know how this book has helped you.

The survey used to compile this book is reprinted in the next few pages. You may choose to complete it for yourself, for curiosity sake. We would appreciate it if you would complete it and return it to us so that we may continue to collect data for future editions of *This Affair is Over!*

Nanette Miner, Ed.D.
Sandi Terri

*Thank you for taking part in this research on women having affairs
with married men. If you have had more than one affair with a married
man, please choose one as representative, and limit the information
you provide to that affair.*
Return to:
BVC Publishing   P.O. Box 1819   Bristol, CT 06011-1819

Part 1   *Background Information.*

Your age at this time _____   Your age when affair started _____
Your lover's age when affair started _____

How did you meet?   _____ friend _____ co-worker
_____ friend of his wife's _____ friend of your husband/boyfriend
_____other

Why did you begin the affair? (check all that apply)
☐ something new and exciting   ☐ to fill a void
☐ boredom   ☐ just sex   ☐ for the chase
☐ attraction   ☐ looking for happiness ☐ conquest
☐ he pursued me relentlessly   ☐ fell in love
☐ other _____

Duration of affair _____ years   _____ months _____ still involved
(provide time *and* check "still involved" if appropriate)

Your marital status at time of affair _____ single   _____ married
_____ single but dating   _____ married but separated   _____ divorced

Your marital status *at this time* _____ single   _____ married
_____ single but dating   _____ married but separated   _____ divorced

How long was your lover married at the time of the *start* of your affair
with him? _____ years   _____ months _____ not married then

Are you now married to, or living with, your lover? _____ yes _____ no

Is your lover still married to the same person? _____ yes   _____ no
_____ don't know

Do you know if your lover has had other affairs? _____ yes _____no
_____ not sure; How many other affairs? ☐ 2-4 ☐ 5-10 ☐ 10+

Have you had other affairs with married men? _____ yes _____no;
If yes, how many? _____

_____

Part 2 *Complete Part 2 whether you're involved in the affair or not; if not in the affair, base your answers relative to that time.*

Has he told you he will leave his wife? _____ yes _____ no

Has he told you he will leave his wife when the following situation occurs (check all that apply):
☐ after the baby is born ☐ my son/daughter turns 18
☐ my son/daughter moves out ☐ my child graduates
☐ we close on our new house ☐ my loan is paid off
☐ holidays are over ☐ fall/winter/spring/summer is over
☐ after our vacation is over ☐ when I have saved X amount of money ☐ other _____

Has he given any of the following excuses (check all that apply):
☐ she won't give me a divorce ☐ too many people will get hurt
☐ I told her I wanted a divorce but she cried
☐ I don't want to hurt her
☐ it will cost me too much money (alimony, child support)
☐ health (his/hers/parents/etc.)
☐ my family/her family ☐ my reputation will be ruined
☐ give me time/be patient ☐ my in-laws paid for.....
☐ I'm afraid she'll commit suicide ☐ the children
☐ I'll lose my job ☐ my religion

☐ other _____

_____

Do you *believe* he will leave his wife? _____ yes _____ no

If currently married, have you considered divorcing your husband?
_____ yes _____ no; To be with your lover? _____ yes _____ no

Do you have children with this man? _____ yes _____ no;
If yes, how many? _____

Have you aborted a child from this affair? _____ yes _____ no;
If yes, how many? _____

Have you tried to end this affair? _____ yes _____ no;
If yes, how many attempts? _____

_____

If more than one attempt, what did he do to win you back?

_____

(fill in briefly)

Are you experiencing, or have you experienced, any of the following related to the affair? (check all that apply):

☐ desperation   ☐ suicidal thoughts
☐ anxiety attacks   ☐ loneliness
☐ distraction   ☐ health problems you attribute to the
relationship   ☐ anger
☐ crying bouts   ☐ vulnerability
☐ depression   ☐ loss of self esteem
☐ loss of control   ☐ feelings of betrayal
☐ other _____

Part 3   Complete Part 3 ONLY if your affair with the married man is over.

Who ended the affair? _____ I did   _____ he did

If he ended the affair, what reason did he give?

_____

If you ended the affair, what was the reason?

_____

If you ended the affair, how many attempts before success? _____

When the affair ended, I felt (check all that apply):

☐ relieved   ☐ happy
☐ acceptance   ☐ determined
☐ self assured   ☐ confident
☐ resentment   ☐ unlovable
☐ used   ☐ I wasted too much time
☐ despair   ☐ angry
☐ stupid   ☐ pain
☐ duped   ☐ suicidal
☐ other _____

Part 4   *Complete Part 4 ONLY if you are/were married to the man that you had the affair with.*

How long had your affair been going on before he left his wife? _____
years _____ months

What actions did he take to end his marriage?
_____ (explain briefly)

Are you still married? ____ yes ____ no   How long have you been
married or how long were you married? ____ years ____ months

Do you believe he has had/did have an affair while married to you?
____ yes ____no

If presently married: do you believe he *will* have an affair while married
to you? ____ yes ____ no

Thank you!